WORLD'S
WEIRDEST
ANIMALS

WORLD'S WEIRDEST ANIMALS

WORLD'S WEIRDEST ANIMALS

MATT ROPER

summersdale

WORLD'S WEIRDEST ANIMALS

This edition published in 2009 by Summersdale Publishers Ltd

First published by Penguin Group (NZ), 2008

Summersdale Publishers Ltd
46 West Street
Chichester
West Sussex
PO19 1RP
UK

www.summersdale.com

Printed and bound in China

ISBN: 978-1-84024-749-7

Substantial discounts on bulk quantities of Summersdale books are available to corporations, professional associations and other organisations. For details telephone Summersdale Publishers on (+44-1243-771107), fax (+44-1243-786300) or email (nicky@summersdale.com).

ABOUT THE AUTHOR

Matt Roper is a feature writer for the *Daily Mirror*. He lived in Brazil for six years, where he managed to survive tarantula attacks, falling coconuts and swimming in piranha-infested waters in the Amazon jungle. He also infiltrated a Bolivian drug gang to investigate child prostitution rings, and dodged bullets to report on death squads in Rio de Janeiro. He returned to the UK after setting up a project for street girls in one of Brazil's biggest cities. He now lives in London with his wife Daniela.

He has written four other books: *World's Weirdest Sports*, *101 Crazy Ways to Die*, *Street Girls* and *Remember Me, Rescue Me*.

CONTENTS

INTRODUCTION...7
PROBOSCIS MONKEY......................................8
DUMBO OCTOPUS...10
AXOLOTL...12
NAKED MOLE RAT..14
STONEFISH..16
STAR-NOSED MOLE..18
TWO-HEADED SHINGLEBACK SKINK LIZARD.........20
HUMPBACK ANGLERFISH................................24
BOULENGERULA TAITANUS.............................26
TEXAS HORNED LIZARD.................................28
LONG-EARED JERBOA....................................30
NARWHAL..32
SLENDER LORIS...34
BUMBLEBEE BAT...36
CANDIRU FISH...40
SAGGY-SKINNED FROG...................................42
THORNY DEVIL..44
BLOBFISH...46
LONG-NOSED ECHIDNA..................................48

AYE-AYE...50

YETI CRAB..52

COOKIE-CUTTER SHARK..56

PHILIPPINE TARSIER...58

FANGTOOTH...60

BLUE-FOOTED BOOBY...62

CAPYBARA..64

OKAPI..66

PELICAN EEL...68

DUCK-BILLED PLATYPUS...72

MATAMATA TURTLE..74

MALAYAN TAPIR..76

EMPEROR TAMARIN...78

LEAFY SEA DRAGON..80

VAMPIRE SQUID...82

MANATEE...84

GIANT PANGOLIN..88

MUSK OX..90

THREE-TOED SLOTH...92

INTRODUCTION

It's a funny old world – hilarious, in fact. Monkeys with eyes the size of saucers, marsupials with huge, rotating ears, naked rats that can sprint backwards... it seems as though some animals have been put on this earth just to make us laugh. Why else would there be lizards that squirt jets of blood from their eyes, porcupines whose teeth are on their tongue, fish whose mouths are 11 times bigger than their bodies, or monkeys with noses so big that they have trouble eating? Not to mention the octopus that looks like Dumbo, the squid that's a dead ringer for Dracula complete with black cloak and glowing red eyes, and the fish with a face like your grumpy great-aunt.

Look around the world and you'll find creatures that you couldn't conjure up, even in your wildest imagination – like the half zebra/half giraffe that cleans its ears with its tongue, the lizard with a false head, or the mole who can gobble down a meal in 230 milliseconds flat. You probably never knew you shared the planet with salamanders that can regrow their own body parts, insects whose young tear off and eat their mother's skin, or rodents that eat their own poo. Turn the page and prepare to be amazed, enthralled, and extremely amused...

PROBOSCIS MONKEY

Nasalis larvatus
LIVES Borneo
EATS Leaves, seeds, fruits, flowers

A huge honker might be a cause of embarrassment for humans, but in the world of the proboscis monkey, the bigger your nose, the more females you can get.

The nose of the male monkey grows so long – up to 17.5 cm (6.9 in.), or a quarter of its body length – that they often block their mouths, making it difficult to eat or drink. But to the proboscis that's just a minor inconvenience – the male with the longest snout in his colony always has the most mates, which can be as many as eight.

Another advantage of having the biggest nose is that they can make the loudest honk in order to frighten off predators – the long nose shoots into a horizontal position with each blast of noise.

The monkeys also have a big pot belly because of the gases released by an extra chamber in its stomach, which helps to digest leaves.

Only found in Borneo, these strange-looking primates hang out in the swampy mangrove forests near the south-east Asian island's rivers and streams. They are expert swimmers, like to dive from the branches of trees as high as 15 metres (49.2 ft), and can stay submerged in the water for up to 30 seconds.

DUMBO OCTOPUS

Grimpoteuthis

LIVES Deep under the Pacific and Atlantic oceans

EATS Crustaceans, worms, bivalves

Just like its famous Disney namesake, the Dumbo octopus has a pair of huge ears, which it uses to 'fly' through the water.

Looking more like the Pokémon Pikachu than a real animal, this cartoon-like creature has developed two fins resembling elephant ears on the top of its head. When flapped Dumbo-style, they can propel the octopus through the water at impressive speeds, and also help it to hover above the sea floor as it searches for snails and worms to eat.

Possibly the deep ocean's cutest inhabitant, this beach-ball-sized invertebrate goes about its business in the black waters of the abysso-pelagic zone, over 4,000 metres (13,123 ft) below the surface of the sea. It can grow up to 20 cm (7.9 in.) in width, and also has glow-in-the-dark suckers on its tentacles, which it uses to attract potential mates.

As many as 37 different varieties of this kind of soft-bodied octopus have so far been discovered, although little is known about most of them, as exploration so deep below the sea has only recently begun.

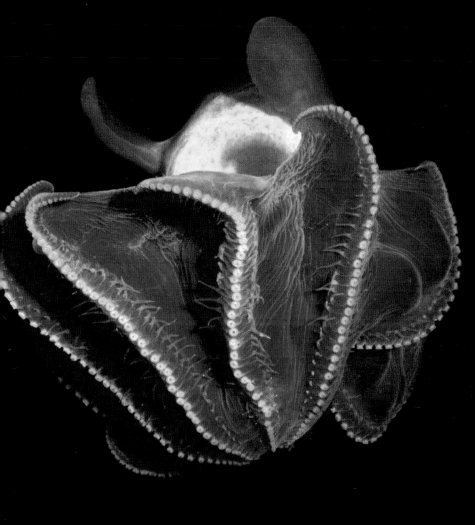

AXOLOTL

Ambystoma mexicanum
LIVES Lake Xochimilco and Lake Chalco in central Mexico
EATS Insect larvae, fish, molluscs

This cheery little creature has a constant grin on its face – and so would you if you could regrow your own body parts.

Not only has the axolotl figured out a way of reproducing its limbs or tail after losing them, it can also regenerate brain and heart cells – an ability that continues to fascinate scientists the world over.

Sometimes known as the Mexican walking fish, the axolotl is actually a type of salamander, although, unlike other amphibians, it never undergoes the change from aquatic to air-breathing creature.

Perhaps because of these amazing powers, legend has it that the axolotl is the Aztec god, Xolotl, who, fearing he would be sacrificed, threw himself into the water and was transformed into the creature we see presently. Today, as in Aztec times, in Mexico the animal is sometimes still eaten or used in medicines. But unlike back then the happy, smiley creature – now on the critically endangered list – is no longer used as a form of currency.

NAKED MOLE RAT

Heterocephalus glaber
LIVES Parts of East Africa
EATS Roots, vegetation, its own faeces

Naked mole rats can run backwards just as quickly as they can forwards. This is just one of the special features these grotesque, hairless rodents have developed for surviving under the ground.

Other useful features include large, protruding teeth for digging, mouths that are sealed just below the teeth to stop their mouths filling with soil, and skin without neurotransmitters so they don't feel any pain – oh, and a peculiar taste for their own (or each other's) poo.

Social colonies of up to 80 naked mole rats live together in complex systems of burrows that can stretch up to 2 km (3 miles) in length. Like termites or ants, each colony has one queen who reproduces, while the other rats have specific functions, such as tunnellers and soldiers. The other females stay celibate so as not to offend the queen – which is why when she dies the fight to take her place can be brutal.

Naked mole rats are the only mammals that are virtually cold-blooded. They also have an extremely low respiration and metabolic rate, so they can survive on the smallest amount of oxygen underground.

STONEFISH

Synanceia verrucosa

LIVES Australia and most of the Indian and Pacific waters
EATS Fish, crustaceans

Cunningly disguised as a piece of seaweed-covered coral, the extremely ugly stonefish simply sits around on rocks or reefs, waits for a tasty fish or shrimp to pass, then gulps it down in just 0.015 seconds flat.

As well as being one of the ocean's fastest eaters, the stonefish is also the world's most poisonous fish – the 13 needle-like spines along its back each have an extremely toxic venom, capable of killing a human in two hours.

An unsuspecting bather who stands on a stonefish will feel pain so excruciating that they can immediately lose consciousness, which is quickly followed by paralysis of the muscles, and finally the heart. Even if the injury isn't fatal, recovery often takes more than six months.

Growing up to 35 cm (13.8 in.) in length, stonefish also sometimes bury themselves in the sand, where they are even more difficult to spot. Amazingly, they can survive out of water for up to 20 hours at a time.

STAR-NOSED MOLE

Condylura cristata
LIVES Canada, eastern USA
EATS Worms, insects, molluscs

The tiny star-nosed mole gives a whole new meaning to the word 'fast food' – it can detect, identify and gobble down a meal in just 230 milliseconds flat.

One of the strangest looking creatures on Earth, this reclusive underground rodent, which is almost completely blind, owes its competitive eating skills to the 22 pink, finger-like tentacles fanning around its nostrils, which transmit touch sensations to the brain.

Although only 1 cm (0.4 in.) across, the fleshy, star-shaped nose contains more than 100,000 nerve fibres – five times as many as run through the human hand – giving them a highly developed sense of touch. High-speed video footage has shown that the tentacles can feel up to ten different objects in a second, and can detect a single grain of salt in a pile of sand.

Scientists recently discovered that the star-nosed mole can even sniff out lunch while underwater, making them the only mammals known to smell through water. The moles blow bubbles through their nostrils, and when one hits an object – like a tasty fish – odour molecules enter the bubble. The mole then sniffs the scented air bubbles back into its nose.

TWO-HEADED SHINGLEBACK SKINK LIZARD

Tiliqua rugosus
LIVES Southern and eastern Australia
EATS Insects, snails, flowers, fruits, berries

It looks like it could bite you at both ends, but one of the shingleback skink's 'heads' is in fact its tail, and is designed to warn off predators.

This stumpy-legged reptile can't move very fast, so when it is being attacked, it waves its tail around as a distraction – and if its tail ends up being bitten off, it will slowly grow back.

So named because its overlapping rows of scales look like shingles on a roof, the rare lizard survives the harsh conditions of the Australian outback because of its unusually thick skin, which protects it from spiky plants and helps retain water in the intense heat. Its tail also contains fat reserves to help it survive the dry season and during hibernation in winter.

Mothers, however, will sympathise most with the female shinglebacks. By the time a baby shingleback is ready to be born, it is a third of the size of an adult – so huge the mother cannot move, breathe properly, or even eat. It is the equivalent of a human giving birth to a six-year-old child.

WEIRD ANIMAL FACTS

Female brown trout will fake an orgasm when they don't want a particular male to fertilise their eggs. Once they have convinced the male he has mated successfully, they will move on to find a better male with which to do the real thing.

Ants of the subfamily Formicinae kidnap the eggs and pupae of other ant species, take them home and raise them as slaves. They spend the rest of their lives doing the foraging, cleaning and babysitting for their masters.

HUMPBACK ANGLERFISH

Melanocetus johnsonii
LIVES Tropical waters of the Atlantic, Indian and Pacific oceans
EATS Fish, shrimp

For many unsuspecting little fish that think they've found a tasty snack, the enormous gaping mouth and long, razor-sharp teeth of the anglerfish are the last things they ever see.

One of the most terrifying creatures of the deep sea, the humpback anglerfish lures its prey using a 'fishing rod' protruding from its head with a luminous tip, which dangles in front of its huge open mouth.

This prehistoric-looking fish, found in the lonely, lightless bottom of the sea over a mile beneath the surface, has watery flesh and light bones, allowing it to hang in the water waiting for passing prey. And the size of prey is no object either – this grotesque creature is able to stretch both its jaw and its stomach to swallow fish up to twice as big as its entire body.

However, only the female of the species is described above. The male is much smaller, looking like a jelly bean with fins. When he finds a female, the male latches onto her with his sharp teeth and becomes a permanent parasite on her body. His mouth fuses with her skin, their two bloodstreams become connected, and eventually he loses his eyes and internal organs, becoming simply a convenient source of sperm.

BOULENGERULA TAITANUS

LIVES In the Taita Hills of south-eastern Kenya

EATS Termites, insects

Forget breastfeeding – *Boulengerula taitanus* babies feed by peeling off their mother's skin and eating it.

The female of this strange African species – a legless, egg-laying amphibian that resembles an earthworm – develops a thick, nutritious outer layer of skin, and her young are born with specialised hooked teeth for tearing it off.

Hatchlings depend entirely on their yummy mummy's skin for as long as four weeks, until their sharper adult teeth develop and they can eat termites and insects, the taitanus' normal diet.

Found only in the Taita Hills of south-eastern Kenya, this unusual creature – which belongs to a group of amphibians called caecilians – lives underground and can grow up to 30 cm (11.8 in.) long. Although the species was first identified in 1935, its unusual parenting methods were only discovered in 2006.

TEXAS HORNED LIZARD

Phrynosoma comutum
LIVES Southern USA and northern Mexico
EATS Harvester ants, termites, beetles, grasshoppers

Looking like something out of *Jurassic Park*, this spiky, scaly reptile also comes with an incredible horror movie-like defence mechanism – it can squirt blood from its eyes to a distance of up to 1 metre (3.3 ft).

Chemicals in the squirted blood make it foul-tasting to dogs, wolves and coyotes. And if, after that, a hungry predator still fancies its chances, the lizard can puff itself up so that spines on its body protrude, making it impossible to swallow.

Found mostly in the unbearably hot deserts of Texas, Arizona and New Mexico, the lizard has also developed an ingenious method of collecting water. As rain begins to fall, it flattens its body, arches its back and lowers its head – water is then channelled through grooves between its scales straight into the corner of its mouth.

As well as being the Official State Reptile of Texas – where it is also known as the 'horny toad', presumably because of its rounded, toad-like body – the Texas horned lizard is also considered sacred by many Native American tribes because it is able to 'weep' tears of blood.

LONG-EARED JERBOA

Euchoreutes naso
LIVES Gobi desert, Mongolia
EATS Insects, seeds, roots

The long-eared jerboa is barely 3 cm (1.2 in.) long, but what it lacks in size it easily makes up for in bizarreness.

This tiny creature looks like a cross between a mouse and a kangaroo, with long, powerful hind legs that allow it to jump up to 1.8 metres (5.9 ft) in a single leap – which is 50 times the height of its body.

Despite being smaller than most people's little finger, it can hop faster than most humans can run, reaching speeds of up to 32.2 km/h (20 mph). And what is more, its ears are twice the size of its head – the largest ear-to-body ratio of any mammal on the planet. Its enormous interceptors help this nocturnal rodent to listen for predators and hunt for insects, its favourite meal.

Like other types of jerboa found in deserts in Africa and Asia, the long-eared jerboa is a solitary animal, each one living alone in its own burrow in the sand. The tunnels of the burrow have only one entrance but several exits, as the jerboas often lightly plug an exit with sand so that they can escape in an emergency.

Amazingly, jerboas never drink. Instead, they gather moisture from the insects they eat, and even recycle moisture from their own exhaled breath.

NARWHAL

Monodon monoceros
LIVES Arctic
EATS Squid, crabs, shrimp, fish

Unique in the world of whales, the narwhal has a front tooth that grows into a long, spiral tusk resembling the horn of a unicorn. In fact, the tusks were sold as unicorn horns in ages past, often for many times their weight in gold. In the sixteenth century, Queen Elizabeth I received a tusk valued at £10,000 – the cost of a castle – believing it came from the head of the mythical horse and possessed magic powers.

However, nobody really knows what the tusk, which can grow up to 3 metres (9.8 ft) long, is used for. Suggested uses have included breaking ice, spearing fish, piercing ships, transmitting sound, poking the seabed for food, wooing females, or defending against a predator.

Recently scientists turned an electron microscope on the tusk and found 10 million nerve endings that detect subtle changes of temperature, pressure, particle gradients and probably a lot more, giving the animal unique insights.

Found only in Arctic waters, the narwhal is among the most vocal of whale species, producing many different sounds, from shrill whistles and high-pitched screams to clicks and low growls. It is even believed that the whale catches prey by stunning it with short bursts of high-frequency sound.

SLENDER LORIS

Loris tardigradus malabaricus
LIVES Sri Lanka, southern India
EATS Insects, slugs, flowers, shoots

With its long, spindly arms and legs and huge, saucer-like eyes, it's no wonder this comical creature got its name from the Dutch word *loeris* for 'clown'.

Found only in a few tropical rainforests of South Asia, the slender loris spends most of its life in treetops, and has specially adapted fingers to help it grasp branches. While hunting, this slow-moving creature can stretch and twist its arms and legs delicately through branches without even slightly rustling the leaves, and can also freeze motionless for hours on end.

While it will eat leaves and flowers if it has to, the nocturnal primate has developed a taste for some of the rainforest's most toxic insects – such as the acacia ant, whose bite can numb a human arm. To protect themselves against the stings of toxic insects and beetles the loris engages in daily 'urine washing' – rubbing urine over its hands, feet and even its face.

While its huge eyes are perfect for seeing at night, they have also helped put the slender loris on the endangered list – local tribes often trap and kill them for use in potions for blindness and eye diseases.

BUMBLEBEE BAT

Craseonycteris thonglongyai
LIVES Western Thailand
EATS Small insects, spiders

Weighing less than a penny and with a head that's just 11 mm (0.4 in.) across, the bumblebee bat is the smallest known mammal.

So named because it is about the size of a bumblebee and is able to hover in mid-air, this tiny creature has a flat, pig-like nose and grows to just 30 mm (1.2 in.) in length. When flying, however, its wingspan can be up to 17 cm (6.7 in.).

Found only in Thailand's Sai Yok National Park, the little bat lives in small holes or crevices in caves, and is most active at dusk, when it flies above the bamboo clumps to feed on insects in flight, or spiders and beetles from the leaves at the top of tall trees.

The species – whose real name is Kitti's hog-nosed bat, after the Thai biologist Kitti Thonglongya, who discovered it – was unknown prior to 1974, but is believed to have been around for more than 43 million years. Now, however, there are estimated to be less than 2000 bats in existence, and because large areas of its forest habitats have been burned, the bat is considered one of the 12 most endangered species on the planet.

WEIRD ANIMAL FACTS

Female house sparrows will sometimes seek out the nest of another female that her partner has also mated with, then kill the female's first young to remove the competition.

North American wood frogs freeze solid in the winter, their heart and brain cease to function, and they can be considered clinically dead. But in the spring they thaw out and come back to life.

CANDIRU FISH

Vandellia sanguinea

LIVES Amazon and Orinoco rivers of South America
EATS Blood of other fish, and occasionally of humans

They may be tiny and toothless, but in the Amazon the candiru is the most feared fish in the water, striking terror into the hearts of men. Why? Well, the clue lies in its other name – the penis fish.

When a man pees in the water, this tiny, eel-shaped fish has a habit of swimming up the urine stream and into his urethra, where it lodges itself by shooting out porcupine-like spikes. Once inside, it is almost impossible to remove except by surgery. The pain is said to be difficult for even the strongest of men to bear, especially as the fish expand in size as they feed on the man's blood and body tissue. Many men die of shock before they get anywhere near a hospital.

Women aren't spared either – the little monsters swim up any orifice they can find. In fact, when natives go in the water to bathe they face the current in order to lessen the chances of one getting in through, er, the back door.

To make matters worse, the eel-like fish, which is just 7.5 cm (3 in.) long and 6 mm (0.2 in.) wide, is translucent and almost impossible to see in the water. And if you give credit to local legend, there's a belief that the strong, fast-swimming fish are capable of swimming up a stream of urine in mid-air to a victim peeing from the shore or a boat.

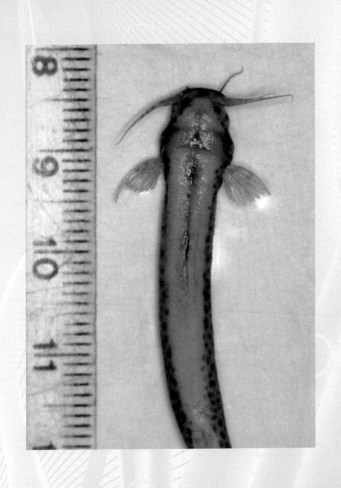

SAGGY-SKINNED FROG

Telmatobius culeus

LIVES Lake Titicaca, on the border of Bolivia and Peru
EATS Fish, snails, crustaceans, tadpoles, worms

It is one of the largest frogs in the world, but the saggy-skinned frog still looks like its skin is several sizes too big for its body.

Found only in Lake Titicaca – the world's highest lake at about 3,800 metres (12,500 ft) above sea level – this crazy frog is covered in baggy folds of loose skin that help it survive the region's freezing temperatures and oxygen-depleted air. In any other environment the same saggy skin would kill it.

Also known as the Titicaca frog, this amazing amphibian – which can grow to 50 cm (20 in.) in diameter – is able to absorb oxygen directly through its skin, and can stay underwater for extended periods of time. So the larger the surface area of skin, the better.

Locals that live around the lake believe the frogs are rainmakers with divine powers, because they have an uncanny ability to know when it is about to rain, coming up to the surface just before a downpour.

Titicaca frogs are also the main ingredient for an aphrodisiacal drink known as Peruvian Viagra. Live frogs are stripped of their skins, then dropped into a blender with water, honey and maca, a local tuber. The disgusting concoction is guzzled by Peruvian men in a show of macho bravado.

THORNY DEVIL

Moloch horridus
LIVES Central Australia
EATS Ants

It may look like a walking piece of barbed wire, but this thorny devil is actually a gentle, harmless lizard – unless you're an ant, that is, in which case it is a cold-hearted, pathological killer. It can scoff as many as 5000 ants in just one sitting.

The reptile only eats one particular species of black ant, and, bizarrely, only one at a time. It often sits by a nest or ant trail for hours on end, using its sticky tongue to flick up the juicy morsels at a rate of 45 a minute.

At home in the harsh Australian desert, the thorny devil makes up for not being able to run or walk very fast by having large, sharp spines all over its body. If a predator still fancies a go, it tucks its head between its front legs to reveal a fat-filled lump rather like a Viking helmet, which makes the creature virtually impossible to swallow.

It can also change its colour to match its surroundings, and can do a pretty good imitation of a dead leaf in the wind by holding its head and tail high above the sand, then lifting each leg slowly as it sways backwards and forwards. If all that weren't strange enough, there's the ingenious way the thorny devil drinks water. Tiny channels between the scales operate like capillaries to carry water up, against gravity, to the corner of the lizard's mouth.

BLOBFISH

Psychrolutes marcidus
LIVES Deep waters off the coasts of Australia and Tasmania
EATS Anything

With a scowl permanently etched on its fed-up-looking face, the blobfish must be the gloomiest, grumpiest-looking creature on the planet. It is also the laziest fish in the ocean, for instead of actively hunting for prey, it prefers to sit around waiting for something edible to float by.

As well as that, its jelly-like flesh is slightly lighter than water, so it doesn't have to expend energy or use scarce oxygen resources swimming or stopping itself from sinking to the sea floor.

Its low-density flesh serves the same function as the gas-filled bladder of most other fish, which would not work 800 metres (2,600 ft) under the sea's surface where the blobfish lives. Here, the pressure is 80 times higher than at sea level.

Rarely seen by humans, scientists don't know much else about the blobfish, but believe it eats anything as long as it can fit it into its mouth. The purpose of its big nose, apart from its comedy value, is also unknown.

LONG-NOSED ECHIDNA

Zaglossus bruijni
LIVES New Guinea
EATS Earthworms, termites

The spiny echidna existed 120 million years ago, making it the oldest mammal on Earth, at one time walking the world with dinosaurs.

Like other mammals, the strange porcupine-like creature is warm-blooded and feeds its young with milk. But unlike other mammals, it lays eggs, has a beak for a head and limbs that stick out from the side of the body rather than underneath – features it has retained from its reptile ancestors. And if that weren't weird enough, the echidna's teeth are on its tongue! With a tiny mouth at the end of its beak and no proper teeth, it compensates by using a set of teeth-like spikes on its tongue to grab hold of earthworms, its favourite food.

Found in New Guinea both in tropical forests and in altitudes as high as 4,000 metres (13,100 ft) above sea level, scientists until recently were baffled at how the long-nosed echidna is able to survive both the extreme cold and heat. The animals can tolerate summer temperatures of more than 40°C (104°F), even though they can't sweat or pant – and lab tests have shown that a body temperature rise to 38°C (100°F) is enough to kill them. However, it is now believed they survive the heat and cold by slowing their metabolic rate, which allows them to go into torpor – a state of regulated hypothermia.

AYE-AYE

Daubentonia madagascariensis

LIVES Madagascar

EATS Insect larvae

The aye-aye gets its name from the cry of alarm most humans make when they see one. And no wonder – with huge, bat-like ears, green Gremlin-like eyes and shrivelled skin, this Madagascan marsupial must be one of the world's creepiest creatures.

In its native forest, superstitious villagers believe the aye-aye, which only comes out at night, brings death to anyone it points its bony middle finger at. The only way to lift the curse is to beat the ugly critters to death, a belief that has put the aye-aye on the critically endangered list.

Despite its uncanny resemblance to Gollum from *The Lord of the Rings*, this tiny tree-dwelling creature is actually a shy, harmless animal that likes nothing more than fishing out insect grubs from inside hollow logs. Using its large, dish-like ears, which can be rotated independently, the aye-aye can detect the slightest squirm of larvae beneath the bark, while its specially adapted skinny middle finger is long enough to reach inside and skewer them like a sausage on a stick. It is the only primate to use echolocation like a bat, enabling it to find grubs up to 2 cm (0.8 in.) deep in a tree.

YETI CRAB

Kiwa hirsuta

LIVES Pacific Ocean

EATS Shrimp, algae

Its furry white looks might make you think it would be more at home in the Himalayas, but this cuddly crustacean – named after the legendary Abominable Snowman – was recently found in the watery deep darkness of the South Pacific.

Spotted by marine biologists in March 2005 about 1,600 km (994 miles) south of Easter Island, this ten-legged creature resembling a crab or lobster is so unusual, a whole new family of animals had to be invented to classify it.

The 15 cm (5.9 in.) long crustacean lives more than 2,200 metres (7,200 ft) below the surface of the sea and is completely blind. It appears to reside around deep-sea hydrothermal vents that spew out fluids that are toxic to many animals.

The purpose of the long, blond hairs that coat its claws is not yet understood, however, the fibres trap bacteria, which the crab may use as food. But some scientists think the hairs may filter out the toxic minerals from the deep-sea vents.

WEIRD
ANIMAL FACTS

Colonies of fire ants survive floods by clinging together to form large rafts that float on the water's surface until the flood recedes, or higher ground is found.

Galapagos marine iguanas can shrink their bodies at will when food becomes scarce. During El Niño conditions, when the algae they feed on decreased, they were found to reduce the length of their bones to make themselves as much as 20 per cent shorter, so they wouldn't need to eat as much.

COOKIE-CUTTER SHARK

Isistius brasiliensis

LIVES All oceans near the equator

EATS Whales, large fish, dolphins

This strange species of shark gets its name from the cookie-shaped wounds it leaves on the bodies of animals much larger than itself.

The small, cigar-shaped fish attaches itself to prey with its sucker mouth, then spins around to cut out a perfectly symmetrical plug of flesh with its razor-sharp, serrated teeth. If that weren't strange enough, hundreds of tiny, light-producing organs on its underside and head cause the shark to glow an eerie green in the deep, dark water.

Found in tropical oceans around the world, the cookie-cutter's body – which can grow to about 50 cm (19.7 in.) in length – has a small black patch on its underside, which makes it look like a small fish to predators such as whales and larger fish, including other sharks. Scientists believe it acts as its own bait, waiting until the predator is about to attack before turning round and attacking its attacker.

They have never been known to attack a person, although a shark once took a cookie-shaped bite out of the rubber sonar dome of a US Navy submarine, forcing it out of service until the damage could be repaired.

PHILIPPINE TARSIER

Tarsius syrichta

LIVES Central and southern Philippines
EATS Insects, birds, snakes

Each of the tarsier's eyes is bigger than both its brain and its stomach – it is the equivalent of a human having eyes the size of grapefruit.

As well as being one of the cutest creatures on earth, this tiny monkey holds the record both for being the world's smallest primate, growing to just 10 cm (3.9 in.) long, and the mammal with the largest eyes. In fact, its saucer-like eyeballs are so huge they cannot move at all in their sockets, so to make up for it, the tarsier can swivel its head 180 degrees in either direction.

Found only in some islands of the Philippines, the nocturnal primate is a shy creature that sleeps during the day in dark hollows near the trunks of trees, and only comes out at night to search for food. It has long fingers to cling to trees and also has an amazing ability to leap from branch to branch for distances of up to 3 metres (9.8 ft) because of special elongated tarsal bones in its ankles – hence the name.

FANGTOOTH

Anoplogaster cornuta
LIVES All oceans of tropical and temperate climates
EATS Crustaceans, squid, other fish

It looks like something from your worst nightmare – but thankfully you won't come across this gruesome-looking fish in real life, unless you happen to be swimming 5,000 metres (16,400 ft) under the sea's surface.

Also known as the ogrefish, for obvious reasons, the fish has an enormous, oversized mouth and the longest teeth of any fish for its size – so long, that it cannot close its mouth completely. And perhaps that is just as well – in the freezing, pitch-black waters of the deep ocean, food comes along so rarely that you have to be able to grab it when it does.

In fact, the two teeth of the fangtooth's bottom jaw are so big that the fish has sockets in the roof of its mouth, allowing it to close its jaws and trap its prey without stabbing itself to death.

However, despite its monstrous appearance, the fangtooth is actually quite small – growing to a maximum length of 15 cm (5.9 in.) – and is harmless to humans. Juvenile fish feed on plankton in the water, only becoming carnivores when they are fully grown. Even then, they are preyed upon by larger fish such as tuna and marlin.

BLUE-FOOTED BOOBY

Sula nebouxii

LIVES Galapagos Islands, Gulf of California, west coast of Mexico

EATS Fish

Its amusing name isn't the only thing that is funny about this comical bird. First of all, it has a very silly dance. Males appear to be particularly proud of their huge, bright blue feet, and to impress the ladies they strut around in circles, lifting their feet high in the air.

If the female is impressed, she then joins in. Both birds stretch their necks and point their bills to the sky, tilt their wings around, then give their mating call. Ironically, the male gives an excited whistle, while the female just groans.

While the booby is clumsy and awkward on land, it is graceful in the air and is specially streamlined for diving into the sea when hunting for fish, from as high 25 metres (82 ft), and has been known to catch fish mid-leap.

One of the reasons why the seabirds were called 'stupid' by Spanish colonisers is that, unlike most wild animals, they have no fear of humans and will happily land on a boat and have a look around – providing an easy meal for hungry sailors. But perhaps the most stupid thing about the booby is that while it likes to eat alone, it actually hunts in flocks. When one bird spots a fish in the sea, instead of going to catch it before any of the others, it gives a whistle to alert the rest of the group, who all dive into the sea together after it.

CAPYBARA

Hydrochoerus hydrochaeris
LIVES Most of South America
EATS Grass, aquatic plants

The world's largest living rodent, the capybara, looks like a giant guinea pig and can weigh more than 45 kg (99 lb). However, it is still tiny compared with its now extinct ancestors, who were larger than the grizzly bear.

These red-haired creatures live along river banks in herds of 10 to 20. They are semi-aquatic, with slightly webbed feet and specially adapted ears that close when swimming. Although they come out on to dry land to rest and bask in the sun, these nervous animals dash straight back into the water at the first hint of danger, and can stay hidden underneath the water for up to five minutes. Capybaras also go into the water to mate and to go to the toilet – and sometimes they even sleep in the water by leaving their noses exposed to the air.

However, their fondness for water has also made them a popular dish. In Venezuela in the sixteenth century, the Catholic Church declared that the rodents were equivalent to fish for the purposes of Lent, making them the only warm-blooded animal that is allowed to be eaten during the 40 days before Easter.

OKAPI

Okapi johnstoni
LIVES Ituri Forest, Democratic Republic of the Congo
EATS Tree buds, leaves

From behind you'd think it was a zebra, but from the front you'd be sure it was a giraffe. Perhaps the weirdest thing about the okapi is that it is the only mammal on earth that can clean its ears with its tongue.

This unusual-looking animal – the sole living relative of the giraffe – is only found in one tropical rainforest in the north-east of the Democratic Republic of the Congo, central Africa, and was unheard of beyond local tribes until 1901. Until then, European explorers had heard stories about what they called the 'African unicorn', but none had managed to see one for themselves.

The okapi is dark brown, except for striking white stripes on its bottom, which are believed to help the young follow their mother through the dense rainforest. The stripes also act as camouflage when the animal is hiding in the partial sunlight that filters through the trees. It has skin-covered horns and long ears that help it detect its predator, the leopard.

Its muscular tongue – which is over 35 cm (13.8 in.) long – can quickly strip the buds and young leaves from trees, but is handiest of all for cleaning those notoriously difficult-to-reach spots, such as underneath the eyelids and inside the ears.

PELICAN EEL

Eurypharynx pelecanoides
LIVES All temperate and tropical seas
EATS Small crustaceans, fish, cephalopods

Another scary monster of the deep sea, the pelican eel is not much more than a giant, swimming mouth with a long tail. In fact, its opened mouth is over 11 times bigger than the rest of its body.

Also known as the umbrella mouth gulper eel, it can unhinge its enormous jaws and stretch its stomach to consume fish much larger than itself. It would be the same as a human being able to gobble down a whole cow.

The pelican eel's whip-like tail, which can be 60 cm (23.6 in.) long, has a glow-in-the-dark red tip which it dangles in front of its mouth to lure unsuspecting prey. Specimens that have been brought to the surface in fishing nets have been known to have their long tails tied into several knots.

And it isn't a fussy eater – food is pretty scarce over 7,000 metres (23,000 ft) under the ocean's surface, so the eel literally gulps down anything that comes along, from seaweed and crabs to squid and octopi.

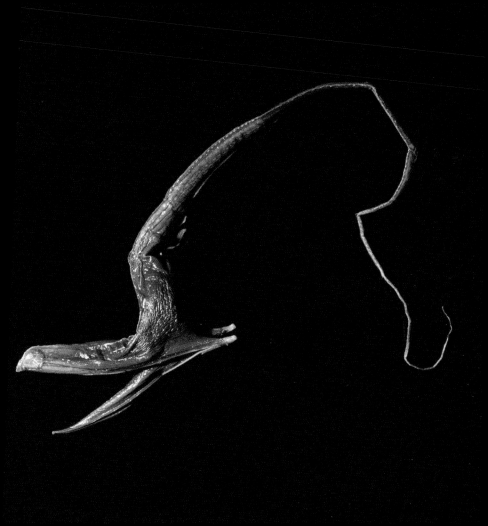

WEIRD ANIMAL FACTS

Swordfish heat up their eyeballs when they are going hunting. The fish has a specially adapted heating organ in the muscle next to its tennis ball-sized eyes, which can raise the temperature to 28 °C (82 °F), even in nearly freezing cold water. Warm eyeballs help them to see prey faster in the murky depths.

The archer fish can shoot a jet of water out of its mouth to knock insects off leaves overhanging the water. It can also predict exactly where the startled insect will land, ensuring it is first to the meal.

DUCK-BILLED PLATYPUS

Ornithorhynchus anatinus

LIVES Australia

EATS Crustaceans, shrimps, worms, insect larvae

So strange is the duck-billed platypus that when it was first brought to Britain in the 1700s, no one believed it was a real animal – people thought someone had sewn a duck's bill on to a beaver's body as a joke. Some of the world's most respected scientists spent months trying to prove that this bizarre creature was some elaborate hoax.

The platypus is one of only three species of mammal to lay eggs, although once hatched, their young feed on their mother's milk, just like other mammals. However, the females don't have nipples, so the milk oozes out of their abdomen, forming pools for the young to lap up.

It is also one of only a few venomous mammals – a pair of sharp spurs on the male's hind foot delivers a poison composed of over 250 different chemicals that is powerful enough to kill smaller animals and cause severe pain to humans.

Unique to Australia, the duck-billed platypus can't move easily on land, but is an excellent swimmer, using its webbed forefeet like paddles and its hind feet like a rudder to help it steer. Spending 12 hours of every day looking for food, its sensitive beak can detect tiny electrical impulses produced by small shrimps and crabs as it searches for food at the bottom of lakes and rivers.

MATAMATA TURTLE

Chelus fimbriatus
LIVES Brazil, Peru, Venezuela, Guiana
EATS Fish

It is one of the oddest creatures you'll ever see – but then again, you'd do well to see a matamata at all, as its bizarre camouflage makes it look almost exactly like a rotten log covered in dead leaves.

In order to vanish into the stagnant pools and swamps where it hunts for prey, the turtle has an extremely flat, triangular head that is covered in bizarre flaps of skin that resemble weeds or algae drifting in the water. It also has a long, straw-like nose that acts as a snorkel, allowing it to breathe while remaining motionless for hours on end underneath the water.

But stranger still is the way the matamata turtle literally vacuums up unsuspecting fish that swim too close to its mouth. The turtle suddenly thrusts out its neck and opens its mouth as wide as possible, creating a powerful suction, which instantly draws the unsuspecting fish inside.

Found in the Amazon and Orinoco river basins in South America, the matamata's shell is covered in horns to protect it from the jaws of the only predator clever enough to find it, the jaguar.

MALAYAN TAPIR

Tapirus indicus

LIVES Thailand, Malaysia, Burma, Sumatra

EATS Shoots, leaves

It looks like a pig with an extremely long nose, but the weird-looking Malayan tapir is actually most closely related to the horse and the rhinoceros.

Found in the dense, swampy rainforests of south-east Asia, tapirs are considered 'living fossils' because they represent an animal group that has changed little over the past 30 million years. One of its unique features is having four toes on the front feet, and only three on the back.

Weighing up to 360 kg (794 lb) and standing nearly 1 metre (3.3 ft) high, the Malayan tapir has the peculiar ability to walk on the bottom of rivers or streams. It also uses its long, rubbery snout – normally used to pull leaves off trees – as a snorkel when it submerges itself underwater to hide from danger.

The animal's distinctive black and white markings also act as camouflage – when foraging at night the tapir blends in with the shadows, and when it is sleeping it resembles a large rock.

EMPEROR TAMARIN

Saguinus imperator

LIVES South-east Peru, north-west Bolivia, north-west Brazil

EATS Fruit, insects, eggs

With its long, white, drooping moustache and sometimes even a goatee beard, the emperor tamarin looks more like an eccentric old man than a monkey. In fact, when Swiss zoologist Goeldi first discovered the funny-looking species in 1907, he was so struck by its resemblance to the German Emperor Wilhelm II, that he named it after him as a joke. The name stuck, and it was even translated into Latin (*imperator*).

But despite their aloof appearance, the monkeys are friendly, playful creatures who leap excitedly through the trees with quick, jerky movements. They spend much of their time cuddling each other, or grooming themselves by combing each other's hair and picking out bugs. In captivity they love to be stroked by hand and will lie on their backs in the hope of having their bellies rubbed.

Emperor tamarins, which are found all over the vast Amazon rainforest, are also unique among monkeys in that their colonies are always led by the oldest female, and when a baby is born all the males take care of it, regardless of which one is the father.

LEAFY SEA DRAGON

Phycodurus eques

LIVES   Waters of western and southern Australia
EATS   Mysid shrimp, sea lice, larval fish

Looking almost exactly like a piece of seaweed floating in the water, leafy sea dragons barely seem to move, as they slowly sway back and forth with the current. They can even change their colour to blend in with the background.

These amazing creatures, which live among kelp-covered rock and seaweed beds, use tiny translucent fins on their back and on the side of their head to swim. Despite appearing lifeless, recent research has shown that they travel hundreds of metres from their home and then return to exactly the same spot, using a well-developed navigation system. They also eat thousands of shrimp and sea lice each day by slurping them up with their tube-like mouths, which work like drinking straws.

But perhaps the most extraordinary thing about the leafy sea dragon is that it is actually the male of the species that gets pregnant and gives birth. During mating, the female lays 100–250 eggs onto a special 'brood patch' on the underside of the male's tail, where they grow to maturity.

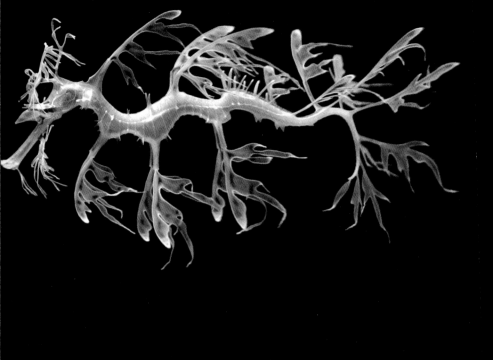

VAMPIRE SQUID

Vampyroteuthis infernalis

LIVES   Temperate and tropical oceans

EATS   Prawns, small crustaceans

It looks like it just swam out of a late-night science fiction movie. With huge, red, glowing eyes, a black, velvety 'Dracula' cloak, and rows of menacing fangs, it's no wonder its Latin name literally translates as 'vampire squid from hell'.

Although it only grows to 15 cm (5.9 in.) in length, this fearsome-looking creature has eyes as big as a large dog's – the largest eyes-to-body ratio of any animal. It also has a pair of arms that can extend to more than twice its body length, which it flaps to 'fly' through the water at impressive speeds – up to two body lengths per second. Even weirder is the vampire squid's strange ability to turn itself 'inside out' to protect itself from predators.

The squid is also covered in light-producing organs called photophores, which give it the unique ability to switch itself on and off like a light bulb. When the photophores are off, the squid is completely invisible in the dark waters where it lives, 3 km (2 miles) under the ocean's surface.

The vampire squid can scare off predators by turning on just two of the bright, disc-shaped lights on the top of its head, making it look like the eyes of a big fish such as a shark. And if that doesn't send them packing, it will spray globs of glowing goo into the water to confuse them.

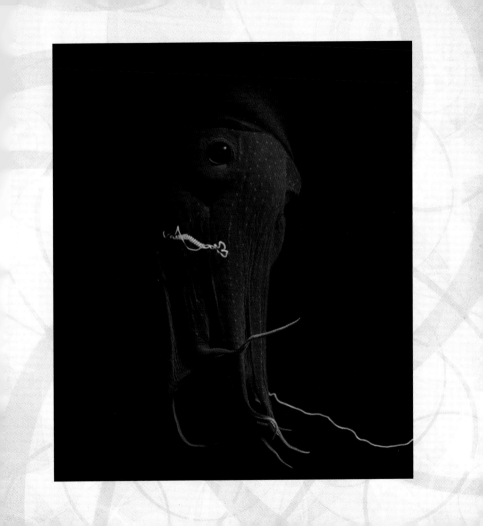

MANATEE

Trichechus manatus

LIVES   Caribbean Sea, Gulf of Mexico

EATS   Sea grass, water hyacinth, water lettuce

While you'd expect the manatee to sink straight to the bottom of the ocean, it is surprisingly agile in the water. And just as well, as its huge body can only be supported in its watery environment – on land its body weight of more than 1,500 kg (3,307 lb) would crush its internal organs.

Most closely related to the elephant, the manatee is the only marine mammal that is a herbivore. In order to keep its big body warm it has to eat up to one tenth of its body weight every day, which means spending up to eight hours a day grazing on aquatic plants, such as sea grass and water lettuce – which is why it is sometimes known as a 'sea cow'. Found in shallow waters no more than 6 metres (19.7 ft) deep, manatees have been clocked swimming at speeds of up to 32.2 km/h (20 mph). They can also renew about 90 per cent of the air in their lungs in a single breath – humans renew only about 17 per cent – enabling them to stay submerged for as long as 20 minutes before having to come up for air.

Because of their size, manatees have no natural predators and can live as long as 70 years. When they are not eating, they like to take part in playful activities, such as 'body surfing' flood control currents, and 'follow-the-leader' in which they all move in single file, synchronising all of their activities, including breathing, diving and changing direction.

WEIRD
ANIMAL FACTS

Humpback whales use their own grammar in the complex songs they sing. During the mating season, males produce love songs to woo the females that combine sounds into phrases, which they further weave into hours-long melodies with recurring themes.

Male king penguins can store undigested food in their stomachs for up to three weeks, a talent unique among vertebrates. The birds produce an antibacterial chemical that destroys bacteria in their stomachs, ensuring the swallowed food stays fresh until it can be regurgitated to feed chicks.

GIANT PANGOLIN

Manis gigantea

LIVES Uganda, Tanzania, Kenya

EATS Ants, termites

The pangolin is the only mammal to have scales instead of hair – except for its eyelashes. Looking like a giant pine cone, the weird animal's stiff, overlapping scales act like a suit of armour, but they are also razor-sharp for inflicting serious injury.

When in danger a pangolin will roll up into a ball, lashing out with the sharp scales on its tail. And if that doesn't send its attacker whimpering off in retreat, it sprays out a foul-smelling liquid from its bottom. A female will even curl up with her baby tucked safely inside.

Also known as the scaly anteater, the giant pangolin sleeps in a burrow during the day and comes out at night to search for ant and termite nests. It uses strong claws to tear open the nests and, using its long, sticky tongue, can devour over 200,000 insects each night.

The largest of eight species of pangolin found in tropical regions of Africa and Asia, it is an extremely solitary creature that doesn't like sharing its burrow, or its ants, with anyone. In fact, only on one occasion has a pangolin been discovered by humans with another pangolin.

MUSK OX

Ovibos moschatus

LIVES Arctic areas of Canada, Greenland and Alaska

EATS Plants, grass

Looking like a walking mop, the musk ox has hair that can grow to almost 1 metre (3.3 ft) in length – the longest of any wild animal – and its woolly undercoat can be as much as 10 cm (3.9 in.) thick.

The musk ox lives further north than any other hoofed animal, and its long hair is essential in helping it survive the long Arctic winters by keeping its body always a few degrees above zero, even if the air temperature reaches −50°C (−58°F). Musk ox fur is eight times warmer than wool and even lighter than cashmere. However, humans have long given up trying to use the musk ox as a source of wool, as the animals would quickly die of pneumonia when shorn.

These huge animals can weigh more than 400 kg (882 lb) and grow to more than 1.5 metres (4.9 ft) in height. They also have two long, thick horns that meet in the middle, creating a type of helmet that has been known to withstand a bullet fired at close range.

When threatened by a predator, musk oxen will first run to a higher location, then turn and stand shoulder-to-shoulder in a circle. With their heads lowered, they form an impenetrable wall. One of the animals may even pick up the attacker with its horns and throw it back into the circle, where the rest of the herd trample it to death.

THREE-TOED SLOTH

Bradypus

LIVES Central and South America

EATS Leaves, buds

Famously slow moving, three-toed sloths travel at a top speed of 0.2 km/h (0.15 mph). However, they only move when they absolutely have to, and spend most of their time hanging upside down from trees, completely motionless.

Because sloths do almost everything hanging upside down – eating, sleeping (an average of 18 hours a day), mating and even giving birth – many of their internal organs, such as their liver, stomach, spleen and pancreas, are in a different position from other mammals, while their fur grows from the belly to the back. They come down from their trees once a week to go to the toilet, but they will wait until it rains to urinate in order to mask their odour from predators.

The reason sloths are so lethargic is because their main food source – leaves – provides very little energy and does not digest easily.

The only time a male sloth shows any get-up-and-go at all is when it's time to mate. Most sloths live alone, so when a female is ready to mate, she lets out a loud, shrill scream, which was thought to sound just like a woman screaming. Any males who hear it, 'quickly' leave their trees and move in her direction – arriving a few hours later. If two males arrive at the same time, they will have an upside down wrestling match until one gives up and leaves, or falls back to sleep.

PHOTO ACKNOWLEDGEMENTS

© TRANZ: Pg 9, 13, 15, 17, 21, 25, 29, 33, 35, 45, 49, 51, 59, 61, 63, 65, 67, 73, 75, 77, 79, 81, 85, 89, 91, 93

© Deep-Sea Photography: Pg 11, 83

© Todd Pusser/naturepl.com: Pg 19

© Alexander Kupfer: Pg 27

© Getty Images: Pg 31, 57

© Merlin D. Tuttle, Bat Conservation International/www.batcon.org: Pg 37

© Peter Henderson, Pisces Conservation Ltd, 2007: Pg 41

© Pete Oxford/naturepl.com: Pg 43

This image has been provided courtesy of the NORFANZ voyage partners – Australia's Department of the Environment and Water Resources and CSIRO, and New Zealand's Ministry of Fisheries and NIWA. For more information on the voyage visit http://www.environment.gov.au/coasts/discovery/voyages/norfanz/index.html. Photo by Robin McPhee and Kerryn Parkinson: Pg 47

© Michel Segonzac: Pg 53

© Doc White/naturepl.com: Pg 69

Have you enjoyed this book?
If so, why not write a review
on your favourite website?

Thanks very much for buying
this Summersdale book.

www.summersdale.com

WORLD'S WEIRDEST ANIMALS